Sacred Vows
THE KNOT OR NOT

LIONEL SHIPMAN

Copyright ©2017 Lionel Shipman

All rights reserved, Except for brief excerpts for review purposes, no part of this book may be reproduced, transmitted, or used in any form without express written permission from the author. Questions and inquiries at Shipmanconsulting.com

This document is protected by the United States Copyright Act, all applicable state laws and international copyright laws. The information in this document is accurate to the best of the ability of the author at the time of writing. The content of this document is subject to change without notice.

Unless otherwise indicated, all Scripture references are taken from the NIV, New International Version: Holy Bible, New International Version®, NIV® Copyright ©1973, 1978, 1984, 2011 by Biblica, Inc.® Used by permission. All rights reserved worldwide. Scripture references are taken from the King James Version of the Bible.

Scripture marked KJV are taken from the New King James Version®. Copyright © 1982 by Thomas Nelson. Used by permission. All rights reserved.

Scripture references marked NLT are taken from the Holy Bible, New Living Translation, copyright © 1996, 2004, 2015 by Tyndale House Foundation. Used by permission of Tyndale House Publishers Inc., Carol Stream, Illinois 60188. All rights reserved.

DEDICATION

Thanks be to God for imparting knowledge, wisdom, and experience to write this book. As God has blessed me, I pray that this book will be a blessing to the readers. All glory, honor, and praise unto God.

To my beautiful, loving, and God-favored wife, Sheila. I cannot imagine my life without you in it. I am grateful to have you as my wife and the mother of our children. I have found a good thing and God has truly favored me. Thank you for saying yes and making our marriage a happily ever after experience. Thank you for your input, encouragement, support, and prayers while completing this book. I love you very much.

To my beautiful and loving daughters, Monica and Camille. Thank you for being the best daughters. God truly blessed us with two great gifts. I love you very much.

TABLE OF CONTENTS

Acknowledgments i

Foreword ii

Introduction v

Chapter 1: The Reality of Marriage 1

Chapter 2: The Path to a Successful Marriage 8

Chapter 3: Communication Builds Commitment 18

Chapter 4: Using this Guide 24

Chapter 5: Family 27

Chapter 6: Lifestyle 45

Chapter 7: Finances 67

Chapter 8: Sex and Intimacy 84

Additional Resources 100

Scripture Resources on Marriage 101

Appendix A: Joint Budget Worksheet 106

Appendix B: Personal Debt Schedule 109

Appendix C: Personal Financial Statement 112

Appendix D: Credit Reports 115

ACKNOWLEDGEMENTS

A special thanks to Ms. Janis Whipple for editing and helping me structure this book. Thank you for your expertise in writing and for the encouragement along the way.

A special thanks to the best couple (Abraham and Rickeyta Snell) anyone could ever have in their life. Thank you for being my brother and sister, counselor, support, and friends over the years. Sheila and I are grateful and blessed to have you in our lives.

A special thanks to my high school English teacher, Mrs. Nellie Sue Helms. Even though I was not fond of writing in high school, you helped create a foundation of writing in my life. Thank you for being the first person to review my initial draft. I appreciate your support and encouragement.

FOREWORD

I have known Lionel for more than 37 years; my wife has known him for about 27 years. He and I have been best friends since the 6th grade, and my wife now considers him a brother to her. Over these past years, my wife and I have developed close, personal relationships with Lionel, his wife, and family. The insightful message contained within this book comes directly from Lionel's heart and experience. It is written with his style - frank, informative, and passionate. For those reasons alone, we could encourage you to keep reading but there is so much more than entertainment in this book. By participating in the practical exercises, you can build a stronger foundation against - and dare we say, avoid entrapment in – the root of many marital issues if you are willing to be honest with your potential mate and most of all yourself.

We live in a time when marriage, family, and indeed society as a whole are experiencing sweeping changes. The foundations of what were societal norms are being challenged on every hand. While this in and of itself is not necessarily bad, it can be quite challenging for those of us who have traditional views on the subject. Indeed, one of the biggest issues in our estimation is the challenge of finding a mate with compatible values, and then raising a family that embodies those values. No two people will always agree in any scenario but add on top of that incompatible value systems and you can get ready for a bumpy relationship. Beyond the beginnings of a marriage and family, we have the fact that people grow and change - sometimes even changing their values system mid-stream. This presents all new challenges to the relationship. This is where commitment, communication, and perseverance all must come to bear. All in all, marriage and family are bedrocks of society but entering these covenant relationships is not for the faint of heart. It takes mature, resolute, flexible, loving, and committed mindsets to make it work for the long term.

It is this reality that sets the landscape for this book. There are no shortages of books on marriage and relationships, written from all kinds of angles, with varying motives. What sets Lionel's book apart from all of those is his ability to not just give advice but to allow you to explore your own psyche and internal motives. By taking you and your potential mate through a set of very telling and emotionally intense questions, his guided instruction helps you to face the realities of marriage and family that go way beyond the infatuation, and in some cases, the fairy tale of the "happily ever after" marriage. With a firm, yet supportive and encouraging approach, the message of this book causes you to answer the "tough" questions of marriage and do so with your potential mate. This may be uncomfortable but growth is rarely comfortable. And that is exactly what marriage is—a process of growth and change.

We strongly encourage every reader to actively engage with what has been placed before you. In doing so, you will provide for yourselves a promising opportunity to experience a marriage that is peaceful, lasting, fulfilling, and happy.

-Abraham and Rickeyta Snell

INTRODUCTION

> *Whosoever finds a wife finds a good thing, and obtaineth favour of the LORD.*
> **Proverbs 18:22, KJV**

As a teenager, I often told my mother I wanted to be married. Marriage was a life goal I was determined to achieve. I loved seeing families together walking in the malls or out eating at restaurants, and hearing the joyful laughter of fathers playing with their children. I admired husbands who opened doors and pulled out chairs for their wives. I enjoyed seeing husbands walking with their wives, hand in hand, as if those moments were the best part of being married.

Not only did I admire other people's marriages but also my parents'. Thankfully they created a beautiful example to follow. Their relationship has not been perfect but it has been special—they have been blessed to celebrate over sixty years of marriage. I admire their long-lasting relationship, which endured many struggles, trials, and hurts but also triumphed with countless victories, positive testimonies, and healings. They have made their marital relationship work. That is what I wanted in my marriage.

I desired to share life with someone—the joys and disappointments, highs and lows, ups and downs, happy and sad moments life brings along. I am blessed to say I have an amazing wife, a great family, a wonderful life, and a whole lot more.

For years I talked to God about my desire to be married. I wanted a beautiful, loving, and fun-filled Christian wife who would love me—all of me. I wanted a relationship with someone who shared similar Christian values and beliefs, a woman who loved God and truly had a heart for people. I wanted someone with whom I could laugh, cry, watch movies, have deep conversations, share success, and build a family and amazing life. I wanted someone who would complement me and add dimension to me as a person (and vice versa). I wanted a person with whom to share equal love, trust, and support. Ours would be a relationship of respect, honor, and friendship.

Through much prayer, studying God's Word, and seeking, I finally found the woman of my dreams, Sheila Smith. It was not love at first sight; however, I knew she was someone special. I was open and interested to discover how life could turn out for us. As I like to describe it, she was a drifting boat out at sea and I was her lighthouse beacon. Of course, she probably tells a different story. She might even say she did not like me at first.

Before meeting one another, Sheila and I had each developed an image of the ideal potential spouse, images we would later need to overcome. Nothing is wrong with having preferences (tall, full-figured, muscular, petite, athletic, dark completion, or somewhere in between) in a potential mate. Just remember, all of us change as we get older. Unfortunately, wrinkles set in, gray hair appears, and energy levels decrease as we age. This is a normal part of life, including married life. Sheila and I realized we needed more than physical preferences to have a long-lasting marital relationship. Therefore, we had to prioritize what was important to us in a marriage (love and companionship, among other qualities). We did not want a shallow relationship; rather, we wanted a relationship to withstand the test of time. We both sought a marital partner with whom we could enjoy life and grow together.

Sheila and I also had preconceived expectations of the person we would marry. While expectations are fine, we had to make sure they were realistic and achievable. Each person entering marriage is far from perfect. Everyone comes into the marriage relationship with some baggage from the past and sometimes the present. We learned to be open about our own individual baggage and past life events, not only to gain knowledge and understand one another but also to help and support each other.

After many months of talking and spending time together, I asked Sheila about dating exclusively. Her answer was funny but serious at the same time. She told me she would have to pray about it. *Pray about it?* I thought. She told me right away she was not playing games and she was taking this part of our relationship seriously because the next steps would lead to marriage. I was serious about dating her exclusively, and although my ego might have been a little bruised, I assured her I wanted the same thing. So I eagerly awaited her response. After about a week, she acquiesced and we were an exclusive happy couple.

> *For this reason a man shall leave his father and mother and be joined to his wife, and the two shall become one flesh; so then they are no longer two, but one flesh.*
> **Mark 10:7–8, NKJV**

Over the next few months we spent a lot of time together, cooking meals and going to entertainment venues, among many other activities. We also spent quality time just talking, getting to know each other, praying together, and discussing many of the areas mentioned in this guide. I cannot recall when it happened—the moment I fell in love with Sheila. I knew she was the one for me and I was the one for her. We decided to spend the rest of our lives together. On March 6, 1999, I asked Sheila to marry me because we were the answer to our individual prayers regarding a mate. Totally opposed to having a long engagement, we immediately chose a wedding date. Five months later, God blessed our wedding on August 7, 1999, and we have enjoyed learning and loving each other ever since. We are living out our happily ever after.

My wife and I often notice elderly couples enjoying life together even after fifty or more years. We see them walking hand in hand as they stroll through the mall or park. I admire how such couples interact with each other and treat each other when on vacation together or even out for a meal or walk. When the opportunity is available, I try to befriend elderly couples to see how long they have been married and ask them the secret to a long-lasting marriage. In these conversations, I always enjoy when the husbands start off in a joking manner:

- Do what your wife tells you to do, if you want any rest.
- Learn to love her cooking.
- The house is hers; remember, you just live there.

After they make us laugh, these couples always give us the real essence of their long-lasting marriages:

- Try to do more for your spouse than they do for you.
- Love and respect each other unconditionally.
- Talk with each other and not at each other.
- Spend time together.
- Do things together.
- Learn from each other.
- Work together.
- Don't go to bed mad with each other.

As with many marital relationships, our relationship has endured some rocky points over the years. My wife and I have had some challenges regarding money, family, and other components of married life that often test marriages. However, because of our early discussions about the subjects in this book, we overcame those challenges through communication and diligence. We learned to work together and not against each other. Even though some of the discussions were difficult because of the subject matter and situations, our relationship has grown stronger and blossomed significantly over the years. Those discussions challenged us to grow as individuals and as a couple. Over the years, we have had far more mountaintop moments than valley moments. Blending our lives into one has been a blessing. We have a great marriage and a beautiful life. I am so glad that we are not alone. Many people have discovered the joy of a successful marriage and an amazing life. You can as well.

Chapter 1

THE REALITY OF MARRIAGE

In today's society, people get married for different reasons. Some marry for companionship and love; whereas others marry for convenience, security, and stability. Whatever the reason, I believe most people who enter into matrimony are looking for a lifetime commitment of love, understanding, companionship, and stability without any recourse leading to divorce. Unfortunately, some marriages still end in divorce. Regardless of how cute couples look or how well they seem to get along in public, divorce is the end result of many marital relationships. Infidelity, lack of passion, lack of communication, or financial mismanagement, among many other things, can cause hurt and disappointment that lead a spouse to call it quits. I often hear men and women say that there is a limit to how much they will tolerate in marital relationships. Many have stated that they can make bad decisions on their own with no help from anyone else. They would rather be divorced or remain single than encounter or tolerate such marital problems.

Marital issues can stem from many areas of life, not just with the most obvious reasons, such as finances or adultery. I know some married couples who are so detached from each other that they live as if they are single.

If a couple fails to do something to salvage their relationship, their marriage is destined to end in divorce.

Unbalanced and Unhealthy Relationships

In some instances, people will place careers, businesses, or other people in a higher priority than their spouses, marriages, and/or families. In this way they take their relationships for granted, meaning they think they can do as they please and always come home to their spouses and families, whom they assume will always be there regardless of separate lifestyles, actions, and activities. Such couples develop an unbalanced or misaligned life together.

Some people devote much more time to one area of their lives and marriages, unfortunately to the detriment of other areas. Relational problems can then surface within the marital life, resulting in imbalance. An unbalanced life is similar to a misaligned vehicle. When a vehicle is misaligned, it causes unnecessary wear and tear on the tires. Excessive wear and tear causes dangerous driving conditions or accidents, which can result in serious injuries or even death. Without proper alignment and balancing, drivers risk their lives every day as they travel on the highways. In life, people risk their marriages and families, among other things, when their lives are out of balance.

Then some people develop negative habits—watching pornography, excessive drinking, gambling, and abuse (verbal and physical)—all of which can destroy a marital relationship. Having such a destructive mind-set and lifestyle can lead anyone to reevaluate and reassess their marital commitment and relationship. Unfortunately in a lot of cases, the end result is a dead relationship and eventually divorce. The committed spouse would rather be alone or with someone else than live under those situations.

In harmful situations, leaving may be the best thing to do. No one should have to live in an abusive relationship. No one should have to live in fear of being controlled by someone else, especially if that someone expresses love with lip service but his or her actions prove otherwise.

Regardless of whether couples are unmarried or married, respect and honor for one another should be exhibited in the relationship. I remember speaking with a young lady slightly older than my daughters about her relationship with her boyfriend. I asked her if the guy respected her. Her delayed response told the truth even before she stated, "Not all of the time." I asked her if the guy was treating her like a queen. Again, her hesitation affirmed what was going on before she uttered the same answer, "Not all of the time." Based on my conversation with this young lady, I concluded that her relationship was not healthy and could lead to some form of abuse, verbally or physically. If this was happening while dating, I can only imagine what would happen throughout their marital relationship. No one deserves to become a victim of abuse of any kind.

Worth Fighting For

Society has made divorce an easy way to avoid the difficult times of marriage. So many people are willing to throw in the towel and give up on their relationships without a fight to stay together. Couples need to consider the time they have invested into the relationship before giving up without any effort to maintain and improve the relationship. I believe many marriages do not have to end in divorce. Couples must be willing to resolve issues and problems to the fullest extent possible before considering divorce. Good relationships are worth fighting for. Some say that their relationships were not good anyway. I ask them, "Did you fight for your relationship?" Problems and issues in marriage are common, but that does not always mean the relationship should end in divorce. Some problems and issues can be worked out and the marriage restored and even improved.

Many people fail to realize two important things regarding divorce: (1) Divorce is not always the answer. (2) Divorce is not always an easy way out of issues and problems. Divorce comes with its own issues and adjustments. Regrettably, some divorced couples wish they could turn back the clock after their divorces. They wish they had spent more time trying to salvage their relationship as opposed to working diligently to dissolve it.

Even in infidelity or financial mismanagement, a marriage can survive through love, forgiveness, faith, honesty, counseling, and effective communication. It takes both, husband and wife, working together to mend the relationship and maintain the bond of marriage going forward. It may take some time, but a broken or unbalanced marital relationship can be salvaged and restored. I personally witnessed a couple overcome and remained married even in the midst of a cheating spouse, though it took many hours of counseling and prayer to rebuild trust in the relationship. The result was worth the effort. Trust is sometimes easier to gain than to restore but it can be done. And marital relationships can survive and thrive.

Happily Ever After?

Marriage is often portrayed in fairy tales as a wonderful life between two people with no problems, arguments, or disagreements...."and they live happily ever after." However, any married couple can tell you this statement is not true.

As a kid growing up, fairy tale stories were common on kiddie television shows and in movies. Many such tales were built on the premise of living happily ever after regardless of the start of the relationship. The woman was either kidnapped or captured by a notorious villain or monster. A courageous man swooped in to rescue and save the fair lady from a dungeon or castle or the grip of a villain. The woman's job was to wait until she was rescued, with hopes of marrying the handsome warrior who fought lions, dragons, and squadrons of villainous men in order to free her. Once rescued and taken back to her kingdom or village, the marriage ceremony took place in the midst of guests from far and near, with all of the decorations and pomp and circumstance imaginable to make the day most memorable. Once the vows were exchanged and they were pronounced husband and wife, after a long passionate kiss they lived happily ever after.

It is amazing none of those TV shows or movies showed us the "happily ever after." One reason could be because it's fictional. Fairy tales leave us with the impression that the happy couple embarks on a life filled only with blue skies every day. That is often the image people have regarding marriage today. Spoiler alert: There will be blue skies some days and dark clouds other days. A couple can have more blue skies than dark clouds in their marriage, but it takes work and commitment.

I recall seeing a talk show some years ago where some of the guests actually believed in "living happily ever after." They believed that once they got married, because of their love for each other, life together would never bring any conflicts, arguments, and/or disagreements. Love would conquer all things. Wake up! Life is not a fairy tale. Life is not a show or movie with predictable outcomes. In the movies, actors and actresses are paid to perform roles. Once the show is over, they go back to their normal everyday lives, which in some cases are anything but normal and happy.

In any relationship, problems will arise and conflict will occur, especially in a marriage. I am not a pessimist. I do believe in having a happy marriage. At the same time, I know that love will not conquer all things in the human sense. It takes more than love to live happily ever after.

Chapter 2

THE PATH TO A SUCCESSFUL MARRIAGE

A couple preparing for marriage may be so starry-eyed about their upcoming wedded bliss that they do not recognize the fallacy of "happily ever after," so they do not prepare for the road ahead. We know the best of marriages will endure challenges as well as joys, especially after the "honeymoon period." But sometimes a marriage may even get off to a bad start in a number of ways. Some people get caught up with emotions and desires around marriage as opposed to investing in a relationship with the person they seek to marry. In so doing, couples learn little about each other before they wed. Some people may know more about relationships in their favorite *television* shows than the person with whom they plan to spend the rest of the lives.

Some people have a sense of entitlement and selfishness in the relationship and are only concerned about their own happiness. Their needs must be met and they're only concerned with getting what they want from the other person. This can certainly start a marriage off on the wrong foot.

Communication

Life does not revolve around the needs and desires of just one person in a relationship. Each person must regard the other's needs and desires and work together so both parties are satisfied in the relationship. The only way to develop this mutual respect and satisfaction is to communicate and spend time with the person you intend to marry. Topics must be addressed. Questions must be answered. And answers must be discussed. After all, this is the person you plan to spend the rest of your life with.

For instance, is the person you plan to marry a spender and risk taker or a financially conservative saver? Does this person prefer a quiet life in the country or a city life? Does your future mate desire to have children or not? These personal choices or preferences are important to discuss as a couple long before walking down the aisle in matrimony. One of worst things that can happen in a love relationship is assuming that the other person shares your same views about life. Make no assumptions. Get to know the person you intend to marry. Do not leave your relationship up to chance. Do not live by the mantra "Love will conquer all." Get to know your future mate. And a couple can only obtain and gather this knowledge by communicating and interacting with each other.

The bible states in Proverbs 4:7 "Getting wisdom is the wisest thing you can do! And whatever else you do, develop good judgment" (NLT). Wisdom is acquired from gathering knowledge (communication) over time. The more couples communicate, the more knowledge and wisdom they acquire about each other (getting to know each other). In addition, communication is not only about gaining knowledge but also resolving areas of conflict and disagreement. As couples communicate, they gain knowledge and learn to understand each other so problems and issues can be resolved more easily.

Married life will not be only a field of lilies and a bed of roses. Life happens. Prepare yourself. There will be many days of joy, happiness, laughter, and excitement. However, some days will bring problems, issues, arguments, and disagreements as well. What makes the difference is the way you handle yourself when these events happen in the relationship. Screaming and hollering at each other, even though it may feel good at such time, or seem to be warranted in a given situation, will not solve problems or resolve conflicts. My wife and I know this is true because the times when we tried it, it never worked. Shouting in anger only compounded the situation and raised the level of frustration, tension, and anxiety in our relationship. Sometimes I shut down and remained silent as she attempted to communicate with me. Other times she raised her voice loudly as I attempted to explain a situation. Neither the silent treatment nor shouting matches bring results. We had to learn and practice a vital key that comes with a successful marriage—effective communication.

Effective communication is essential in a marital relationship and in most other relationships. However, effective communication should begin well before walking down the aisle. As couples spend time together talking and interacting with each other, their relationship grows and their love for each other begins to blossom. At this stage, couples decide to continue toward marriage or continue as friends or go their separate ways.

A successful marriage takes more than love. It takes will, commitment, determination, motivation, and compromise. My wife and I had to learn each other's likes, dislikes, habits, ambitions, passions, and routines, among many other things. I had to learn what makes my wife happy and what disappoints her. My wife had to learn what places a smile on my face and what brings a frown. The only way to learn these signals is through communicating and interacting with each other. We had to communicate effectively in order to bring love, trust, commitment, understanding, joy, and companionship into our marriage. We discovered that the more we communicated, the better we understood each other. That does not mean we do not have problems, issues, or conflicts from time to time. However, because we learned to communicate effectively with each other, conflicts are resolved much easier and problems are solved more smoothly.

By communicating well, my wife and I have developed a greater level of respect for each other. As the years have passed, we have grown closer to each other, and our marital bond and love for each other have grown stronger and deeper. Do we still have disagreements? Yes, but because we talk to each other and not at each other, we are able to come to a mutual agreement and work out any issue or problem. Through effective communication, our marriage has solidified a relationship with a firm foundation of love, trust, and understanding. We are not only husband and wife; we are best friends. We have not perfected our relationship, but we have built a firm foundation upon which we constantly build.

Investment Begins before the Marriage

Over the years, we realized that marriage is what we make it, so we had to invest in our relationship. Our investment comes through communication and interacting with each other. Just as people invest in financial options such as stocks and bonds or mutual funds, they must invest time and effort in their marital relationship. When they do, the value of their marriage increases. Over time, along with minimizing the risks (negative outside influences and anything that works against the relationship), the investment increases in value, which leads to a successful marriage. The greater the investment, the greater the return. My wife and I want a successful marriage, and we are determined to do so by investing in ourselves individually and in our marriage collectively.

As we've stated, investing in each other and the marriage means communicating and learning about one another before you say, "I do." Learning about your potential spouse can resemble the events leading up to the merger of two companies. When two companies decide to merge together, a number of activities must take place, such as meetings, conference calls, and site visits. It is vitally important that the companies communicate and get to know each other outside of accessible public information. Management teams from both companies are tasked with learning the operations of the company as a whole as well as each business unit or subsidiary. They conduct a market analysis of the products and services of each company. Every department is examined to determine any overlap or duplication of activities. The corporate culture and any community involvements are evaluated. Often every position within the company is reviewed and measured. Each team also analyzes the financial history and outlook of each company. All of these endeavors must be completed to determine whether a combined company will be more viable and successful than each individual company will be independently. The only way to know is to learn through effective communication. The coming together of a couple works in a similar fashion. Through communication, the two will learn about each other before walking down the aisle to determine if they have the potential together for a successful marriage.

Benefits of Marriage

A successful merger of two companies may bring about many benefits, such as a broader array of employee perks—discount offerings to entertainment venues, shopping, and travel are just a few. Other benefits might include free education to obtain bachelor's and master's degrees or specialized certifications. Being part of a larger company can provide more room for career growth, better health care, improved technology, as well as other benefits.

A strong marital relationship also comes with benefits. One of the biggest benefits my wife and I enjoy is companionship and support. There is nothing like sharing life moments with the person you love the most. Regardless of the environment, time, or place, I enjoy sharing my life with my wife. Whether a meaningful conversation about religion, politics, society or education; or a vacation in the Caribbean or on the West Coast; or just enjoying family time and watching a movie or television show or singing and dancing together—companionship is a great benefit in our marriage.

There is nothing like a supportive person to encourage you when you are down and cheer you when you are up. My wife and I have each other's backs through the struggles and joys of life, and this trust is based on love and respect. We never openly or directly embarrass or humiliate each other. We never allow other people to slander, hurt, or defame each other, especially in our presence. Never ones to condone fighting, we know if we had to defend one another, we would do it in a heartbeat.

My wife was supportive when I was laid off of work due to company consolidation several years ago. Losing your means of employment can be a serious blow to a man's self-esteem and character. I was devastated when it happened to me. I felt so inadequate and was worried because I was the primary breadwinner of our family. My wife supported me with her encouragement and prayers. She helped me find other employment. She shared with me the effects of losing my employment. Another time in our marriage, my wife was ill due to some health problems. As she supported me when I was out of job, I supported her during the hospital stay and recovery. Regardless of any life event we face as a couple, we stand firmly together through the tears, frustrations, and eventual victory. That is the way couples should relate to one another in a marriage. My wife and I look forward to growing old together as supportive companions.

Marriage Is Like Doubles Tennis

Here is my wife's and my philosophy on marriage. If a person is unwilling to share with a spouse or soon-to-be spouse in one area of life, such as finances, he or she may not be willing to share in all areas of life. If one is not willing to disclose fears or weaknesses, he or she may not be willing to disclose other important areas of life. This will hinder or even hurt a marital relationship. Couples must be willing to share in all areas and to communicate openly and honestly with each other. Couples should be able to talk about all their hurts, fears, ambitions, goals, disappointments, worries, and pet peeves. That is why effective communication within a relationship, especially marriage, is so important. Without effective communication a marriage consists of confusion, chaos, unnecessary mistakes, misguided assumptions, and problems.

My wife and I share, in all areas of our marriage, our innermost hearts without the worry of being ridiculed or chided. I know she loves me, will protect me, and has my best interest at heart. She knows I love her, will protect her, and equally have her best interest at heart. We view marriage as a partnership, where both of us contribute 100 percent to the relationship.

I like to compare marriage to a game of tennis, particularly doubles. Unlike a singles game, where players rely solely upon their skills and abilities to win, doubles tennis relies on the skills and abilities of both partners to win the game.

> Two are better than one, because they have a good return for their labor.
> **Ecclesiastes 4:9, NKJV**

My wife and I have to rely on each other and must trust each other. At times one person must pick up the slack when the other is not playing well in the relationship. This is common in marriage. There will be times when the other person is not playing well. Keep in mind, the goal is to win together. It takes both people to win a successful marriage. A word of caution: If a person tries to play the whole court or game without involving the other partner, that other player may feel inadequate, alone, or worse yet, angry. This could pose problems and arguments in a marriage. Again, effective communication is the key to eliminating problems and being successful in a marriage.

Couples must realize that in marriage they are no longer playing a singles game. Rather, it is a doubles game "til death do us part." Each person has something to contribute to the marital relationship and should be allowed to do so. Each has strengths and weaknesses, ideas and suggestions, different views and perspectives. Each has skills, experience, knowledge, feelings, and emotions. Some people may contribute more in one area than another. However, collectively the combination of these contributions balances the marriage, but only through effective communication.

Couples must learn from each other and work together through communication to make the marital relationship stronger and successful. It takes both persons fulfilling their roles and responsibilities and working together to make a successful and fulfilling marriage. Remember, winning together is the goal.

Chapter 3

COMMUNICATION BUILDS COMMITMENT

Before moving forward with reading this guide and completing the work, take a deep breath and release it slowly. You may be a survivor of a relationship that ended badly or amicably. Whatever caused your past relationship to end is in the past. You made it. You are here in the present. Consider this time in your life as a starting point. Thank God you have the opportunity to start afresh.

Some people must begin again by asking for forgiveness and forgiving those who may have trespassed against them. If this is you, do it now so you can move forward with your life now. You have permission to leave the past in the past. Release yourself from past hurts, mistakes, and fears. Live with no regrets. Today is a new day in the rest of your life. Start fresh with a renewed mind, heart, and spirit. Change the areas of your life that need to be changed. Get in the starting blocks again and get ready to run.

Crucial Areas of Communication

This book is a useful, resourceful tool for couples seeking to be married. Whether you are walking down the aisle for the first time or remarrying, the questions you will consider in four crucial life areas will help provide a foundation of effective communication. It should not be your only guide to marriage but be used in conjunction with premarital counseling, which I highly recommend to all couples seeking to be married.

Every marriage is different because every person is different. However, the common areas of life discussed in chapters 5–8 can make or break a relationship. There are no guarantees that a marriage will last a lifetime. However, effective communication in these four areas (family, finances, lifestyle, and sex & intimacy) can minimize and limit the chances of divorce because it focuses on creating a strong foundation for the relationship before walking down the aisle.

Some people entered a previous marriage with their eyes partially or completely shut, it seems, meaning they did not really get to know their spouse before walking down the aisle. Many may have been infatuated with a partner's looks, careers, or other desirable trait, but did not get to know the person regarding *life*. They did not spend quality time discussing past upbringings, ambitions, goals, likes, and dislikes. They never really engaged in deep conversations around family, lifestyle, religion, or politics. Some were more concerned with how their spouse would be satisfying to them sexually. Some were more concerned with outward appearance as opposed to the inward reality of the person they planned to marry. Some enjoyed the dinner engagements, parties, activities, and entertainment without getting to know the person's heart when there were no events to attend. Rarely did they have a discussion about children, education, and careers. Because their relationships did not start on a good foundation, marital bliss became in some cases marital hell.

Each person comes into a relationship with beliefs, values, habits, endeavors, and passions. I believe the four areas of this guide will open the door of communication between couples to learn about and understand each other. This communication will help create a foundation that both parties can build together. My wife and I are a testament of discussing these vital areas of life. Effective communication in these areas has greatly improved our marital relationship.

Communication Takes Commitment

Marriage is a God-ordained union held in high regard and is purposeful. It is not for everyone, but for those who seek marriage, do not take it lightly. It is a life commitment that requires diligence and patience.

> Marriage is honorable among all.
> **Hebrews 13:4, NKJV**

This guide was written to help couples build a foundation through effective communication. Does it have all of the answers? No. Does it address every issue or problem? No. I have not found or read the perfect relationship book or guide that addresses every issue and provides answers to every problem. I am sharing what has helped my marriage, what keeps my marriage intact and healthy. Those of you seeking to be married, do not be deceived into thinking your love will conquer everything—every problem, situation, or circumstance in a relationship. There will be times when it seems, looks like, and feels as if love is dwindling, but because of your commitment, among many other things, your relationship can survive and weather the storms of life. There will be times when you may not like your spouse—their ways and habits—during the relationship. Because of love, commitment, and temperance, among many other qualities, your marriage relationship can prosper and endure the test of time.

My wife and I believe there is no mountain we cannot climb and no river we cannot cross. With God's help we can overcome any obstacle. Any successful marriage takes love, work, dedication, commitment, submission, understanding, temperance, and sometimes compromise. And these can best be established through effective communication, as you'll be encouraged to develop through the chapters and exercises that follow.

You may have talked with others who gave you their thoughts regarding marriage. However, you are your own person. Not that you cannot learn from others, but you must come to your own conclusions regarding marriage. Therefore, be open to the material and questions in this book. Some people may not have had a question or a topic come up to this point in their relationship, but this guide discusses some situations that likely will come into your life in one way or another. It is best to discuss these subjects and discover now what your potential spouse believes. And see if you can come together on common ground before walking down the aisle.

Love and Trust

My hope is that you and your potential spouse will have the highest regard for each other; that you will find comfort in each other; and that there will be no topic or subject off limits, no area of life that you cannot be open and honest about. Hopefully you will be able to validate each other without judging one another. I hope this book not only makes you a better couple but better people individually, not only as a spouse but a parent to your (future) children and a friend and family member to loved ones in your life. I hope you will become more loving and more open to share your heart with people, and they can do the same for you, not only in your marriage but throughout your life.

My hope is that you understand that the love you share with your potential mate will not conquer all but will help you work through the issues of life. It may not be the primary driving force for every issue, but that love for each other makes the process a lot easier. At times you will have to truly trust the guidance of your spouse, even when you do not fully understand. But your love and trust for each other will help secure your relationship, whatever the outcome. And most importantly, trust God in your marriage. He created the foundation of marriage, and who better to trust in your marital relationship. May God bless you as you utilize this guide in your relationship and future marriage.

Chapter 4

USING THE GUIDE

Note: This book can assist not only couples seeking to be married for the first time, but also those who are seeking to marry again or who are currently married.

I recommend couples set aside time and schedule at least two hours a week (one-hour sessions) to discuss the four sections of this guide. However, before any discussion, each person should read and complete the four sections separately. Once each person completes the reading and the answers in each section, schedule an hour of uninterrupted time to review and discuss one section at a time. That means spending at least an hour on each area. Some sections may require more time and attention than others, depending on the couple. It is vital that couples complete the work separately. Only during your scheduled review and discussion will you reveal your individual responses to each other.

Please note: The finance section requires additional attention and work. At the end of this guide, there are instructions on how to obtain your individual credit reports (see appendix D). Each person must obtain a copy of all three reports and be willing to share and review all of the reports with each other during the scheduled time. Also, the three financial worksheets at the end of this guide must be completed (appendix A: Budget Worksheet, appendix

B: Personal Debt Schedule, and appendix C: Personal Financial Statement Short Form), but only the personal debt schedule and the personal financial statement short form should be completed individually prior to the scheduled meeting. During your scheduled meeting time, the two of you will utilize your individual personal debt schedules and work together to create a joint budget after you've completed the guide (see budget worksheet, appendix A). Some of the information on the personal debt schedule, along with other documentation from your monthly expense statements, such as utilities, receipts for gas and food, etc., will be used to complete the joint budget worksheet. The personal financial statement can be used to determine your net worth and should coincide, from a debt obligation standpoint, with the personal debt schedule. Once you are married, utilize this joint budget worksheet or a similar budget worksheet, software, or application as a starting point in your combined finances going forward. You decide the method that works best for you.

Even though the point of this guide is to encourage effective communication among couples seeking to be married (first time and previously married), it can also be used to refresh existing marital relationships. I believe it is important to invest in your relationship throughout your marriage. Just as you take steps to improve your fiscal investment in order to yield a better return, you should jointly invest in your marriage to yield a better relationship.

At times during the course of completing this guide, a third party such as a counselor or advisor may be needed to help couples understand and clear up unresolved issues. This can be addressed with the person(s) providing the premarital counseling.

The next four chapters address four key areas that couples should focus on to improve their relationship and build a solid and successful marriage. Even though there are other areas, this book will focus on the following four areas: family, lifestyle, finances, and sex/intimacy.

I pray and hope this guide is helpful in providing a foundation of effective communication in your future or present marital relationship.

Chapter 5

FAMILY

Family is defined as a fundamental social group in society, typically consisting of one or two parents and children. It can also be defined as two or more people who share goals and values, have long-term commitments to one another, and reside usually in the same dwelling place. In regard to marriage, each person must know a potential spouse's views, values, and goals of family and family life.

Part of discussing family life is being willing to reveal each other's values, morals, and ethics. This knowledge helps you truly understand the person with whom you plan to spend the rest of your life. There is a saying that opposites attract. This is not always true. A person's ideas about family may cause one to choose to marry someone of similar views as opposed to opposite beliefs. For example, a person who prefers not to exhibit affection, such as holding hands, embracing, or kissing in public, may not want to marry someone who embraces public affection in a relationship, especially a marital relationship. Another example could be a person who enjoys hosting family or friends at their home. This could pose a problem in a marital relationship if the partner prefers their home time to be for the family only.

I was raised in a rather large household compared to my wife's family. There were seven siblings in my parents' family and three in my wife's family. During our courtship, we discussed having children. Based on my upbringing, I wanted a large family, meaning I wanted at least four to five kids; however, my wife only wanted two kids. This could have been an area of contention had we not discussed having children before we got married. I met a couple who had a rough time in their marriage because the husband did not want to have children but the wife did. Well, roughly fifteen years into their marriage, the wife became pregnant. She was so excited about having the child. However, her husband did not share the sentiment. She stated that the pregnancy was not planned but it happened. The couple really struggled in their marriage during the entire pregnancy.

Being in a relationship can bring challenges and struggles simply because of the personalities of each partner. In addition, from time to time there will be challenges from family, friends, and other outside relationships that invade a couple's relationship, directly or indirectly. Sometimes, these challenges can become a thorn in a relationship and cause disagreements and contention within the marriage. From nosy and domineering in-laws to money-seeking siblings and family members, couples often have to deal with decisions whether or not to intervene or let nature take its course. Due to these challenges and issues, couples must discuss life events and family circumstances before the wedding ceremony.

As seen on one of my favorite television shows, *The Brady Bunch*, blending two families can be exciting but also present a number of challenges. In the Brady family, a man with three sons and a woman with three daughters came together as one combined family. Before a couple with two families enters into remarriage, the subject of blending the families should be discussed. The couple must openly deal with the integration of the kids into the new family, step-parenting, how to get along, and how to respect each other and accept each other as family.

This section will address a number of questions that revolve around family and family life in a marriage. Couples should review and answer the following questions separately and discuss their answers together.

Why are you getting married? Or, if already married, why did you marry the person you are with? Please discuss.

_____
_____
_____
_____
_____
_____
_____
_____
_____
_____

What are your expectations of marriage?

_____
_____
_____
_____
_____
_____
_____
_____

How do you feel about divorce? Share your thoughts and views. Please discuss.

_____
_____
_____
_____
_____
_____

What are your experience(s) regarding divorce? How did it affect you? Please discuss. If not applicable, please state N/A.

_____
_____
_____
_____
_____

Any previous marriages? ____ If so, how and why did it end? Please discuss.

_____
_____
_____
_____
_____
_____
_____

Do you desire to have children? ____
How many?_____ Please discuss.

_____
_____
_____
_____
_____
_____
_____

If you both desire children, and infertility becomes an issue, are you open to adoption or foster parenting? Discuss.

_____
_____
_____
_____
_____
_____

Should you decide to have children, will you be equally involved in their lives? _____ Discuss how you prefer to share parenting responsibilities.

_____
_____
_____
_____
_____
_____
_____

Will one of you stay home or will the child or children stay in childcare/daycare? Please discuss.

_____
_____
_____
_____
_____
_____
_____

Do you or your potential spouse have children? _____ How many? _____

_____
_____
_____
_____
_____
_____
_____

Will the children live with you? _____ If not, how often will they visit? _____ Please discuss.

_____
_____
_____
_____
_____
_____

What role or responsibility will you or your partner (as a stepparent) have in disciplining the child or children? Please discuss.

_____
_____
_____
_____
_____
_____

If you are or your partner is a stepparent, what role or responsibility will you have with the child's or children's biological parent(s)? Please discuss.

_____
_____
_____
_____
_____
_____

What forms of discipline do you approve and what forms do you disapprove? Please discuss.

_____
_____
_____
_____
_____
_____

What roles will your parents, your spouse's parents, and/or your siblings, (i.e. grands, aunts/uncles, as applicable) play in your marital relationship? Please discuss.

_____
_____
_____
_____
_____
_____

How often or when will you visit your parents and other family members? Please discuss.

_____
_____
_____
_____
_____
_____

How often or when will they visit you?
Please discuss.

_____
_____
_____
_____
_____

When marital problems occur, will you consult with your parents, siblings or other people? ____
Please discuss.

_____
_____
_____
_____
_____
_____
_____

Will you spend holidays with each other's parents or other family? ____ If so, how will you divide your time between your parents and family and your spouse's family? Please discuss.

_____
_____
_____
_____
_____
_____

(Recommendation: Create your own traditions for the holidays.)

_____
_____
_____
_____

Will you consider taking in a parent or loved one (such as for health reasons or financial needs)? Please discuss.

_____
_____
_____
_____
_____
_____

Discuss household responsibilities and duties such as cooking, cleaning, yard work, etc.

_____
_____
_____
_____
_____
_____

If there are conflicts within your parents' family, what is your role and responsibility? Please discuss.

_____
_____
_____
_____
_____
_____
_____

If you and your spouse's friends do not currently have cordial relationships, how will the both of you handle interaction with them after you're married?

_____
_____
_____
_____
_____

Do you have any anger issues?

_____
_____
_____
_____
_____
_____

What happens when you get upset? Please discuss.

_____
_____
_____
_____
_____
_____
_____
_____
_____
_____

How do you deal with conflict? Personal? Work? Please discuss.

_____
_____
_____
_____
_____
_____
_____
_____
_____
_____

When marital disagreements occur, how will you solve them? (I recommend establishing rules for engagements beforehand, such as agreeing to never embarrass one another in public.)

_____
_____
_____
_____
_____
_____
_____
_____
_____
_____

Do you have a problem with forgiveness? _____
Discuss how you handle forgiving others and asking for forgiveness.

_____
_____
_____
_____
_____
_____
_____
_____
_____
_____

Are you willing to help family members who are in need (financially)? ____ Please discuss.

_____
_____
_____
_____
_____
_____
_____

What causes do you contribute your time and resources to, if any? List.

_____
_____
_____
_____
_____

Will you continue to support those causes? Please discuss.

_____
_____
_____
_____

What will you do if your spouse does not support one or some of these causes? Please discuss.

_____
_____
_____
_____
_____
_____

Will you seek to have work-family balance? How do you envision you and your spouse creating this balance? Please discuss.

_____
_____
_____
_____
_____
_____
_____
_____
_____
_____
_____

Do you work long hours (beyond forty hours a week)? ____ If so, if your long work hours interfered with your marital/family relationship, what would you do? Please discuss.

_____
_____
_____
_____
_____
_____
_____
_____

Are there things in life you would withhold from your spouse? _____ If so, what are they?

_____
_____
_____
_____
_____
_____
_____
_____

Will your future spouse have access to your computer, email, mail, etc? ___ Please discuss.

_____
_____
_____
_____
_____

Which area(s) of family do you think will be the biggest challenge in your marriage and why? How can you prepare to face this challenge positively so that it does not negatively affect your marriage?

_____
_____
_____
_____
_____
_____
_____
_____
_____
_____
_____
_____
_____
_____
_____
_____
_____
_____
_____
_____
_____
_____
_____
_____

ADDITIONAL NOTES

Chapter 6

LIFESTYLE

The way people lived yesterday can positively or negatively affect the way they live today and tomorrow. Because of this, relationships can be influenced positively or negatively. Having a unique or different lifestyle may be an attraction to some people but not others. This reminds me of a reality show I heard about where couples from different and sometimes strange backgrounds come together to be married. They are required to spend time getting to know each other only for a short period of time before exchanging vows. During each episode, viewers are shown the interaction and reactions of the man and woman as they spend time as a new couple. Some of the couples appear to be fine with their partners' strange behavior and activities, whereas others will not compromise or accept the strange behaviors.

Activities such as smoking marijuana and using other recreational drugs may be accepted by some but not all. Men and women are often pulled into trying drugs like these or worse in a new relationship. However, some men and women will not tolerate even an experimental try of any drugs. To some people, drinking and excessive partying, smoking, or gambling are noncompromising activities in a marital relationship.

Other lifestyle areas must also be addressed before walking down the aisle, such as religion and politics. Even though these viewpoints can be emotionally sensitive to some people, it is good to know the political, religious, cultural, and societal views of your future partner. You must decide how any marked differences between you might affect the relationship long-term.

It is true that opposites can attract, but that does not mean two totally opposite people are meant to be in a marital relationship. A person's views of life and society may not be a problem or a cause of conflict with a person in a platonic or friendly relationship, but it could most definitely in a marital relationship. Some partners will not accept certain viewpoints from a spouse in a marital relationship. Some beliefs and activities may be tolerable in a friendship but not in a marriage. Therefore, couples need to determine what is acceptable and what is not, what is agreeable and what is not. Some couples have areas of life where they agree to disagree, while at times one or the other person has certain deal breakers that could cause major problems in a marriage, either now or down the road.

Nontraditional or other religious beliefs could become a major factor as to whether or not a person will enter into a marital relationship with someone. Also, the lack of believing in God can be a huge determinant as to whether or not a person decides to spend his or her life with that special someone. Religion creates and shapes the foundation of a person's life and is highly regarded in a relationship, especially in a marital relationship.

Marrying someone with different religious beliefs or no beliefs is not an option for some people. This area must be addressed before walking down the aisle.

Do you believe in God? Are you conservative? Are you footloose and fancy-free? Do you follow the rules in life? Are you career driven? Are you a risk taker? The answers to these questions could possibly determine whether you should marry the person you are with or keep looking for a potential spouse with similar answers to your own. Your fiancé or significant other's lifestyle could initially be a primary attraction for you, but it may not be what you would want in a husband or wife. Over the years, I recall hearing some people (men and women) say that there are two types of people: one for enjoyment and the other you bring home to your mother. In this case, the one you bring home to your mother is the person you marry.

Note: For married couples, if there are some major differences regarding your lifestyles, you really need to communicate with each other. It is vitally important to live a married life understanding how both of you are going to live together. Remember, marriage is similar to a doubles match of tennis. You are not in a singles game anymore.

This section will address a number of questions that revolve around lifestyles in a marriage. Couples should review and answer the following questions separately and discuss their answers together.

Are you a homebody? If so, how do you like to spend time at home? If not, how much time do you spend at home?

_____
_____
_____
_____
_____

Do you like to socialize? If not, what would you be willing to do to compromise if your spouse likes to socialize? If you do, what kind of socializing is important to you and why?

_____
_____
_____
_____
_____
_____

Are you involved in any organizations or activities that may be questionable to others? _____ If so, which ones and how are you involved?

_____
_____
_____
_____

_____
_____
_____

Do you have or have you ever had any major illness or disease (i.e., cancer, diabetes, heart or kidney disease)? _____ If so, describe the history or present condition.

_____
_____
_____
_____
_____
_____
_____

Have you ever had any surgeries? _____ Please list.

_____
_____
_____
_____
_____
_____
_____

Do you have now or have you ever had any issues with substance abuse (i.e., nicotine, caffeine, alcohol, or drugs of any kind)? _____ If so, please discuss.

_____
_____
_____
_____
_____
_____

Do you use any recreational drugs such as marijuana? _____ If so, how often and how much?

_____
_____
_____
_____
_____
_____

Do you smoke or drink? _____ If so, how often and how much?

_____
_____
_____
_____
_____
_____

Do you gamble? If so, how often? How much money do you allocate to gambling?

_____
_____
_____
_____
_____

Do you have a criminal background? ____
If so, please discuss in detail.

_____
_____
_____
_____
_____
_____

Are you willing to submit to a criminal background check? ____ Why do you think this question is important, or do you?

_____
_____
_____
_____
_____
_____
_____

Have you ever struggled with any mental or emotional problems? ____ Please discuss.

_____
_____
_____
_____
_____
_____

What are your thoughts on suicide? Please discuss.

_____
_____
_____
_____
_____
_____

What are your beliefs regarding abortion? Please discuss.

_____
_____
_____
_____
_____
_____
_____
_____
_____

Have you ever had an abortion or paid for an abortion? _____ If yes, please discuss.

_____
_____
_____
_____
_____
_____
_____

What are your hobbies and activities? List.

_____
_____
_____
_____
_____
_____

How will you integrate your extracurricular activities or hobbies into your married life? Please discuss.

_____
_____
_____
_____
_____
_____

If these activities or hobbies limit family time, are you willing to decrease time spent on them? Please discuss.

_____
_____
_____
_____
_____
_____
_____

How important is it that you share some hobbies or interests with your spouse? How can you do this?

_____
_____
_____
_____
_____
_____

Do you utilize social media? If so, what platform(s) and how often? What is the purpose or reason for use?

_____
_____
_____
_____

Are you a gamer? If so, how often do you play video games? What type of games do you play?
_____
_____
_____
_____
_____
_____
_____

Are you politically active? ____ If so, how? Please discuss.
_____
_____
_____
_____
_____
_____
_____

Which political party are you registered with? Why? Please discuss.
_____
_____
_____
_____
_____
_____
_____

Do you exercise? ___ How often? ___

_____
_____
_____
_____

Is health important to you? ___ Please discuss.

_____
_____
_____
_____
_____
_____

How would you feel if your spouse gained or loss an excessive amount of weight, twenty pounds or more? Please discuss.

_____
_____
_____
_____
_____
_____

How would you feel if your spouse changed his or her appearance (i.e., tattoos, hair, piercings, surgery, etc.)? Please discuss.

_____
_____
_____
_____
_____
_____
_____

How important is it that your spouse approve of your appearance or fitness level?

_____
_____
_____
_____
_____
_____

What are your career aspirations?

_____
_____
_____
_____
_____
_____

If your career aspirations include continuing your education, how will it affect your relationship (for example, time needed for class and study, financial cost, or relocating)? Please discuss.

_____
_____
_____
_____
_____
_____
_____

If traveling is a part of your career, will you continue to travel and how often are you willing to travel? _____ Please discuss.

_____
_____
_____
_____
_____
_____
_____
_____

What shift do you work? _____ Depending on the shift, how will that affect your time you spend with your spouse?

_____
_____
_____
_____
_____
_____
_____
_____
_____
_____

How well do you get along with your fiancé's family? Please discuss.

_____
_____
_____
_____
_____
_____

If there are issues with your fiancé's family, how will you resolve them? Please discuss.

_____
_____
_____
_____
_____
_____
_____

How will you balance your current friendships and your marriage? Please discuss.

_____
_____
_____
_____
_____
_____
_____

What do you feel about your spouse continuing platonic friendships with the opposite sex?

_____
_____
_____
_____
_____
_____
_____

How important is it that the two of you have separate friends and or couples' friendships?

_____
_____
_____
_____
_____
_____

Are you okay with your spouse going out with their single friends? Please discuss.

_____
_____
_____
_____
_____
_____

Do you have pets? ____ If so, what kind?

_____
_____
_____
_____

What pets are absolutely out?
_____
_____
_____
_____
_____

Does your fiancé like pets, and is he or she willing to live with your pet or pets? _____ Please discuss.
_____
_____
_____
_____
_____
_____

How important is cleanliness (house, car, personal hygiene, etc.)?
_____
_____
_____
_____
_____

How important is timeliness? Please discuss.
_____
_____
_____
_____

How important is having organization and structure in a marriage relationship?

_____
_____
_____
_____
_____
_____
_____

What religion or faith are you a part of? Please discuss.

_____
_____
_____
_____
_____
_____

Do you practice what you believe? Please discuss.

_____
_____
_____
_____
_____
_____
_____
_____

Are you fine with your partner being a nonbeliever or being an atheist or agnostic? Please discuss.

_____
_____
_____
_____
_____
_____
_____

Will you go to church together or separately? _____
If separately, why? Please discuss.

_____
_____
_____
_____
_____

Which area(s) of lifestyle do you think will be the biggest challenge in your marriage, and why? How can you prepare to face this challenge positively so that it does not negatively affect your marriage?

_____
_____
_____
_____
_____
_____
_____
_____
_____
_____
_____
_____
_____
_____
_____
_____
_____
_____
_____
_____
_____
_____
_____
_____
_____

ADDITIONAL NOTES

Chapter 7

FINANCES

The topic of money and financial matters has been discussed in various publications, seminars, and media outlets for many years now. Finances always have been and will forever be a hot topic of discussion—on television news shows, around water coolers in corporate offices, in countless books—and lived out by all, whether people have a lot of it or not. Regardless of a person's background, socioeconomic status, age, or education level, money is discussed among all people. The rich talk about maintaining and investing money, the poor talk about getting some of it, and those in between talk about making more of it and how not to lose what they have acquired thus far. It is such an important topic because it affects everyone, including married couples. It is a widely held belief that a high percentage of marriages end in divorce due to financial matters. Therefore, it is important to address money and finances with couples seeking marriage because of their different backgrounds with money, perspectives of money management, and outcomes of being fiscally responsible or irresponsible.

Some people spend money "like there is no tomorrow"; others save with little to no enjoyment in life. Some people are frugal; others are huge givers. Financial perspectives can vary from person to person. Some were raised to be financially responsible and taught how to manage money. Others were brought up in a household of financial irresponsibility and poor money management skills. Because of wide ranges of money perspectives, I recommend that couples (both those seeking to be married or already married) address their individual points of view regarding money as well as their understanding of money management.

Over the years, my wife and I have helped married couples who were on opposite sides of the subject of money. They needed assistance because most of these couples never took the opportunity to discuss their understanding of money before marriage or even after they were married. They made many assumptions in their relationships. In most cases, the women assumed that their husbands knew how to manage money, and the men assumed that their wives knew how to balance the bank account. They never communicated about their individual understanding of money. Instead, they argued a lot and had a rough time agreeing on major money issues. Most of the time these financial issues landed couples in marriage counseling. I can recall one instance, as I assisted a young couple, when the wife turned red from frustration over a financial decision her husband made without telling her. In fact, she was unaware of this decision before they met with me. She was so upset that she wanted to leave. He just placed his head down on the table in tears. Thankfully, my wife and I were able to help them with their money issues, but we had to recommend that they seek marriage counseling.

In a relationship, couples must be willing to admit it if they know little about money. What one does or does not know about money is nothing to be ashamed of, even if one partner has more knowledge and money-management experience than the other. The crucial issue is communicating about the subject of money *before* it becomes a problem in the relationship. When couples come together and communicate their understandings, experiences, strengths, and weaknesses of money management, married life is made better. Disagreements and misunderstandings will still occur from time to time. However, effective communication reduces and limits these potential conflicts.

Communication about money matters in a relationship is also not a one-time priority. Couples should talk about financial matters often. My wife and I come together once or twice a month for what we call a pow-wow session, where we discuss what has transpired, what is currently going on, and what lies ahead regarding money. These meetings allow us to stay in touch and stay on track with our goals, thoughts, and concerns around money.

This section will address a number of questions that revolve around finances in a marriage. Couples should review and answer the following questions separately and discuss their answers together.

What kind of money manager do you consider yourself to be and why?

_____
_____
_____
_____
_____

What did you learn about money management growing up, positively or negatively?

_____
_____
_____
_____
_____

Who handled the money in your family when you were growing up, and how much did you hear about it as a child or teenager?

_____
_____
_____
_____
_____

What financial misunderstandings, if any, did you have after you left home and how did they affect your financial circumstances?

_____
_____
_____
_____

Do you set financial goals? _____ Why or why not?

_____
_____
_____
_____
_____

What are your financial goals?

_____
_____
_____
_____
_____
_____

How do you plan to work toward these goals?

_____
_____
_____
_____
_____
_____
_____
_____

Do you currently have debt? _____
What kind and how much?

_____
_____
_____
_____
_____
_____

Have you ever filed bankruptcy? _____ If so, why? Please discuss.

_____
_____
_____
_____
_____

How is your credit history? (I suggest each person pull a copy of his or her individual credit reports to verify credit activity. See appendix D for instructions. Do this once or twice a year hereafter.)

_____
_____
_____
_____
_____
_____
_____
_____

How much does each of you earn?

_____
_____
_____
_____

Do you have a problem with your spouse making more money than you? Please discuss.

_____
_____
_____
_____
_____
_____

Will you have separate or joint bank or loan accounts? ____ Why? Please discuss.

_____
_____
_____
_____
_____
_____
_____
_____

Are you comfortable with a joint budget? ____ If not, please discuss. (See instructions and sample budget worksheet in appendix B at the end of this book.)

_____
_____
_____
_____
_____
_____
_____
_____

Are you comfortable with your income and expenses? ____ Please discuss.

_____
_____
_____
_____
_____
_____

If you are not happy with your current income and expenses, what plans do you have to change them?

_____
_____
_____
_____
_____
_____
_____

What will happen if either of you go over a joint budget? Please discuss.

_____
_____
_____
_____
_____
_____
_____

Who will manage the accounts to pay the monthly expenses? Please discuss.

_____
_____
_____
_____
_____
_____
_____

How much can you or your spouse spend without consulting the other? Please discuss.

_____
_____
_____
_____
_____
_____
_____

Do you plan to invest? ___ Why or why not? Stocks?___ CDs?___ Mutual Funds?_____ Real Estate?___ Please Discuss.

_____
_____
_____
_____
_____
_____

Discuss your retirement plans.

_____
_____
_____
_____
_____
_____

Do you like to shop? ___ How often do you shop? ___
What is your shopping weakness?

_____
_____
_____
_____
_____
_____
_____

At what dollar amount should you have a conversation with your mate about a potential purchase?

_____
_____
_____
_____
_____
_____
_____

Will major purchases be joint decisions and paid jointly? ___ If not, why not? If so, how do you plan to come to joint decisions?

_____
_____
_____
_____
_____
_____
_____

Do you believe in tithing? ____ Do you give tithes and offerings regularly to your church?____ Why or why not? Please discuss.

___
___
___
___
___
___

Do you give charitable contributions to other organizations?____ If so, why and which organizations? If not, do you have a problem if this is important to your spouse? Please discuss.

___
___
___
___
___
___

How will you finance vacations? Credit card? Loans? Cash? Please discuss.

___
___
___
___
___
___

How often do you eat out? Please discuss.
_____
_____
_____
_____
_____
_____

Do you gamble or play the lottery? ____
How often? ____ How much do you spend? ____
_____
_____
_____
_____
_____
_____

Will your wedding preparations, including honeymoon, put you further in debt? Please discuss.
_____
_____
_____
_____
_____
_____
_____
_____

How much are you willing to spend on your children's activities such as sports, etc.? Please discuss.

_____
_____
_____
_____
_____
_____
_____

Do you believe you are totally responsible for your children's college costs? Please discuss.

_____
_____
_____
_____
_____
_____
_____

As you continue working and are given pay raises along the way, what are your plans for pay raises? Please discuss.

_____
_____
_____
_____
_____
_____
_____

Will you have an emergency fund? If so, how much, and what will it be used for? Please discuss.

_____
_____
_____
_____
_____
_____
_____

Which area(s) of money management do you think will be the biggest challenge in your marriage, and why? How can you prepare to face this challenge positively so that it does not negatively affect your marriage?

ADDITIONAL NOTES

Chapter 8

SEX AND INTIMACY

> The husband should fulfill his marital duty to his wife, and likewise the wife to her husband. The wife does not have authority over her own body but yields it to her husband. In the same way, the husband does not have authority over his own body but yields it to his wife.
> **1 Corinthians 7:3–4**

My wife and I believe that sex and intimacy is God-given and should be experienced only during marriage between a man and a woman. Sex and intimacy are so important in a marriage. Just as money used to be taboo but is now more openly discussed among marital couples, so have sex and intimacy become easier to communicate about between people in a relationship. Just as money is a crucial subject to discuss, both before and after the wedding, couples must also communicate about sex and intimacy in their relationship. Misunderstandings about sex and intimacy, or not enough of it in a relationship, may cause issues or problems in a marriage.

> Do not deprive each other except perhaps by mutual consent and for a time, so that you may devote yourselves to prayer. Then come together again so that Satan will not tempt you because of your lack of self-control.
> **1 Corinthians 7:5**

On the other hand, a marital relationship requiring an overabundance of sex may have similar results. Lack of sex could lead a spouse to seek it from another source (adulterous affairs, prostitution, pornography, etc.). Unfortunately, this occurs often in marriages across the world. We see it glamorized in movies and television shows as if it is alright. However, there are reasons such actions are counseled against and addressed by the Bible as wrong. Infidelity can lead to broken hearts and broken lives, in addition to divorce.

Pornography in particularly negatively affects the person involved, but also the marital relationship in a number of ways. A person can grow to feel that his or her mate's appearance is not good enough for the marriage. People engaging in pornography, some men specifically, want their spouses to look more physically appealing by requesting physical enhancements (breast implants, etc.) or weight loss, or requesting that their wives wear exotic, sexy clothing or experiment in sexual fantasies. Pornography can cause the mate to feel unloved and inadequate because they do not measure up to the other person's expectation. It can also cause a strain in the marriage because of the money needed to support a pornography habit or addiction. Websites, videos, and other methods of pornography can be costly and negatively affect the marriage emotionally, spiritually, and financially.

Sex and intimacy is new for some couples, meaning they have not had any sexual experiences outside of marriage. However, some couples may have had a number of experiences before they met and during the dating stages of their relationship, or they may have been married previously. Because of past experiences, or the lack thereof, sexual and intimacy issues or problems may arise during marriage. There may be some things in your past that could have affected your view of sex and intimacy. Therefore, it is vitally important to talk about this subject before you take those marriage vows.

Unfortunately, we live in a world where sexual pressure is prevalent for both men and women. Men sometimes pressure women into premarital sex, and vice versa. It seems to give the person a sense of control over the other, but in actuality, pressuring a partner for sex before marriage is a selfish act. Society has become open to premarital sex and often endorses it, even encourages it, much like a person should test-drive a car before purchasing it or kick the tires first.

Another crucial area of discussion for couples before marrying is sexual aggression. In any relationship, a person enters with some form of baggage. Granted, some of the baggage may be heavier than others. Either person could have a history as a sexual abuse victim. Either person could have been a victim of a sexual aggressive partner or ex-spouse or could have been the perpetrator. While some past experiences may not have been classified as sexual assault, the perpetrator's actions were aggressive and sometimes frightening. It is vital that the couple have a discussion regarding each other's past sexual histories. Be willing to seek professional counseling or help if either of you has unresolved emotional or mental issues related to past experiences with sexual aggression or abuse.

In addition to sexual history, couples need to discuss other areas of marital intimacy and romance. By definition, *intimacy* means "a state of being marked by emotional closeness; something that is private and personal." Intimacy, romance, and sex are all interconnected in a marriage, so couples need to communicate about all aspects of this area of their relationship, including both the physical and emotional elements of intimacy.

It is important that couples learn and understand each other's physical drives when it involves intimacy. My wife always uses the phrase "Scratch me where I itch," which means to do things that will satisfy her. The only way we were able to learn "how to scratch each other where we itched" individually was through communication and respecting and honoring each other from an intimacy and sexual standpoint. We learned that sometimes intimacy, which could be whispering sweet nothings in each other's ear or setting the stage for a romantic evening, did not always lead to sex. There were times when we would just share our deeply regarded thoughts or feelings with each other. At other times we enjoyed a great evening of pleasure. Either way, over time we became emotionally tied together. We know each other's most intimate thoughts and have built a great level of trust in each other. Las Vegas has a commercial stating that what happens in Vegas stays in Vegas. We feel the same way regarding our intimate relationship. So should your relationship remain a private connection, but remember to communicate well about sex and intimacy so you can enjoy this area of your life together.

This following section will address a number of questions that revolve around sex and intimacy in a marriage. Couples should review and answer the following questions separately and discuss their answers together.

How would you define intimacy in a marriage relationship?

_____
_____
_____
_____
_____
_____
_____

How important is intimacy to you? How important do you think it is to your spouse? Please discuss.

_____
_____
_____
_____
_____
_____

How would you define romance in a marriage relationship?
_____
_____
_____
_____
_____
_____

How important is romance to you? How important do you think it is to your spouse? Please discuss.
_____
_____
_____
_____
_____
_____
_____

What does romance from your spouse mean to you?
_____
_____
_____
_____
_____
_____
_____

List and discuss the specific things and/or activities that are romantic to you.

_____
_____
_____
_____
_____
_____
_____
_____

Are you willing to show romance to your spouse even if it is not your way?

_____
_____
_____
_____
_____
_____
_____

Is physical contact (holding hands, hugs, kissing, etc.) important to you?

_____
_____
_____
_____
_____
_____
_____

What are your expectations in giving and receiving gifts for birthdays, Valentine's Day, Christmas, and other days or occasions? Please discuss.

_____
_____
_____
_____
_____
_____

What do you expect from your partner regarding sex and intimacy? Please discuss.

_____
_____
_____
_____
_____
_____

Discuss your past sexual experiences, if any. Include partners (same or opposite sex), number of partners, and type of sex.

_____
_____
_____
_____
_____

Have you ever had partners who were sexually aggressive? How did that affect your future relationships and your attitude toward sex and intimacy?

___

Have you been sexually aggressive in the past toward a partner? If so, why? What do you need to do to make changes for this relationship?

___

Do you have any history of sexual abuse? ____ If so, did you receive therapy? ___ How do you think it will affect your sex life once you get married? Please discuss.

___

Have you ever committed any sex crimes? ___ If so, please discuss. Have you been a victim of a sexual crime? ___ If so, please discuss.

_____
_____
_____
_____
_____

Have you ever had any sexually transmitted disease? ___ If so, please list.

_____
_____
_____
_____
_____
_____

How often would you like to have sex? Please discuss.

_____
_____
_____
_____
_____
_____
_____
_____

What is okay and what is not okay sexually?
Please discuss.

_____
_____
_____
_____
_____
_____

Do you think pornography is okay? Please discuss.

_____
_____
_____
_____
_____

Communicating what you need from your partner sexually is important. How comfortable are you with discussing your sexual needs with your partner? Please discuss why you may or may not be uncomfortable doing so.

_____
_____
_____
_____
_____
_____
_____

What makes you happy during sex and intimacy? Please discuss.

_____
_____
_____
_____
_____
_____
_____

Do you believe in having an open marriage where other people (man or woman) are involved sexually in the marriage? Please discuss.

_____
_____
_____
_____
_____

How will you feel about the times your spouse may not feel like having sex? Would it make you feel unloved or would you understand? Please discuss.

_____
_____
_____
_____
_____
_____
_____
_____
_____
_____

For men: It may take several weeks or a couple of months before a woman can have sex after childbirth. It is advisable for any man to be considerate and patient as his wife recovers. In addition to recovering from the physical aspect of childbirth, some women may face postpartum depression, which could hinder sexual activity. Please discuss.

_____
_____
_____
_____
_____
_____
_____
_____
_____

There are many life phases in marriage, especially when kids are brought into the relationship. Because of the time and attention required to raise children, there is a tendency to limit romance and sexual activity in a relationship. The demands of work, business, childcare, and life obligations can often cause couples to neglect their needs and desires for romance, intimacy, and sex. Couples should make time for themselves even if it means scheduling sex. Please discuss as a couple how you will manage and balance your time with each other, especially your intimate time, and the other areas of your life—children, work, and other aspects of life.

_____
_____
_____
_____
_____
_____
_____
_____
_____
_____
_____
_____
_____
_____
_____
_____

Which area(s) of sex and intimacy do you think will be the biggest challenge in your marriage, and why? How can you prepare to face this challenge positively so that it does not negatively affect your marriage?

ADDITIONAL NOTES

ADDITIONAL RESOURCES

Because communication is so integral to a marriage relationship, it is important that couples seek additional assistance from time to time to ensure that their relationship continues to grow and sustain throughout the journey of the marriage. For further assistance and guidance in relationships, I recommend that couples read *The 5 Love Languages: How to Express Heartfelt Commitment to Your Mate* by Dr. Gary Chapman (Chicago: Moody Publishing, 1992). It addresses the five areas in which people commonly express love: words of affirmation, acts of service, receiving gifts, quality time, and physical touch. Understanding these areas will affect a couple's relationship and intimacy. Personally, the book has been a great help to our relationship. It is important that each person in a relationship discuss their needs and desires in each of the five areas.

I also recommend that couples read *Love and Respect: The Love She Most Desires; the Respect He Desperately Needs* by Dr. Emerson Eggerichs (Nashville: Thomas Nelson, 2004). My wife and I really enjoyed this book because it provided a clearer understanding of the unconditional love and respect that couples should exhibit in a marital relationship based on God's Word.

SCRIPTURE RESOURCES FOR MARRIAGE

Throughout your marriage, the following Scriptures can be used in conjunction with prayer about your marriage. All the way back to Genesis, God was the one who created the marriage relationship. The health and the well-being of your marriage depends upon you and your spouse's investment in the relationship. There is no better investment than God's Word through prayer.

The LORD God said, "It is not good for the man to be alone. I will make a helper suitable for him." Now the LORD God had formed out of the ground all the wild animals and all the birds in the sky. He brought them to the man to see what he would name them; and whatever the man called each living creature, that was its name. So the man gave names to all the livestock, the birds in the sky and all the wild animals. But for Adam no suitable helper was found. So the LORD God caused the man to fall into a deep sleep; and while he was sleeping, he took one of the man's ribs and then closed up the place with flesh. Then the LORD God made a woman from the rib he had taken out of the man, and he brought her to the man. The man said, "This is now bone of my bones and flesh of my flesh; she shall be called 'woman,' for she was taken out of man." That is why a man leaves his father and mother and is united to his wife, and they become one flesh.

Genesis 2:18–24

⁴ "Haven't you read," he replied, "that at the beginning the Creator 'made them male and female', [a] ⁵ and said, 'For this reason a man will leave his father and mother and be united to his wife, and the two will become one flesh'[b]? ⁶ So they are no longer two, but one flesh. Therefore what God has joined together, let no one separate."

Matthew 19:4–6

The institution and foundation of marriage is accredited to God, not man. Seeing that He created marriage, He knows all about it. Trusting in God's Word through prayer and application continues to provide answers to problems and resolutions to issues in my marriage. Blessings flow freely in our marital relationship. Because God is not a respecter of persons, He can do the same for your marital relationship.

Submit to one another out of reverence for Christ. Wives, submit yourselves to your own husbands as you do to the Lord. For the husband is the head of the wife as Christ is the head of the church, his body, of which he is the Savior. Now as the church submits to Christ, so also wives should submit to their husbands in everything.

Husbands, love your wives, just as Christ loved the church and gave himself up for her to make her holy, cleansing her by the washing with water through the word, and to present her to himself as a radiant church, without stain or wrinkle or any other blemish, but holy and blameless. In this same way, husbands ought to love their wives as their own bodies. He who loves his wife loves himself. After all, no one ever hated their own body, but they feed and care for their body, just as Christ does the church—for we are members of his body. "For this reason a man will leave his father and mother and be united to his wife, and the two will become one flesh." This is a profound mystery—but I am talking about Christ and the church. However, each one of you also must love his wife as he loves himself, and the wife must respect her husband.

Ephesians 5:21–33

Let this be a reminder that it's not about doing what your spouse says, but what the Bible encourages both of you to do. Husband and wife must love, honor, and respect each other. We must be accountable to one another in our roles and responsibilities. Do this: treat each other the way God treats you individually. If you strive to treat each other the way God treats you, your marital relationship can only blossom into a beautiful life.

Marriage should be honored by all, and the marriage bed kept pure, for God will judge the adulterer and all the sexually immoral.

Hebrews 13:4

Although our society believes it is socially acceptable to just live together as a couple, I am a believer in the sanctity of marriage. As the Bible states, marriage is honorable and should be honored among all people. There is nothing like seeing a couple living a life of commitment and dedication to each other in matrimony.

Now for the matters you wrote about: "It is good for a man not to have sexual relations with a woman." But since sexual immorality is occurring, each man should have sexual relations with his own wife, and each woman with her own husband. The husband should fulfill his marital duty to his wife, and likewise the wife to her husband. The wife does not have authority over her own body but yields it to her husband. In the same way, the husband does not have authority over his own body but yields it to his wife. Do not deprive each other except perhaps by mutual consent and for a time, so that you may devote yourselves to prayer. Then come together again so that Satan will not tempt you because of your lack of self-control.

1 Corinthians 7:1–5

May your fountain be blessed, and may you rejoice in the wife of your youth. A loving doe, a graceful deer— may her breasts satisfy you always, may you ever be intoxicated with her love.

Proverbs 5:18–19

I am a believer that love, intimacy, and sexual pleasure, which were created by God, are for the enjoyment between a man and woman within the confines of marriage. Both should honor and respect each other's needs and desires.

He who finds a wife finds what is good and receives favor from the Lord.

Proverbs 18:22

I am a bit old-fashioned for a reason in this regard. I believe that the woman is the prize in a relationship, which supports this scripture of a man finding a wife and gaining favor from the Lord. The man is happy because he finds a good thing and the marital union is blessed of God. I knew that I found a prize when I married my wife. And, I have enjoyed having the prize in my life ever since. Couples should learn to feel the same way in their marriage.

Appendix A

JOINT BUDGET WORKSHEET

Complete the budget worksheet together by combining each other's income and expenses. This will require a little work because you must utilize some information from the debt schedule as well as information from your monthly expense statements such as your utilities, cable, and cell-phone bills, etc. Enter the amounts on the line items that are applicable, then add your income amounts together and add your expense amounts together. Once all of the amounts are entered, subtract your total expenses from your total income (Total Income – Total Expenses = Income After Expenses). If the number is positive, you have a surplus (net income). If the number is negative, you have a deficit (net loss). If you have a surplus, allocate the amount as shown in the line items of the budget worksheet.

Category	Month #1	Month #2	Month #3
Income (+)			
Income #1			
Income #2			
Total Income			
Expenses (-)			
Tithes/Offerings			
Mortgage/Rent			
Electricity/Heat			
Water/Sewer/Trash			
Internet/Telephone/Cellphone			
Food/Supplies			
Auto payment/Insurance			
Auto Gas			
Entertainment			
Cable/Satellite			
Loans			
Credit Cards			
Miscellaneous			
Total Expenses			

Income After Expenses			
Allocation:			
Savings			
Emergency Fund			
Retirement Account(s)			
Pay Down Debt			

BUDGET NOTES

_____
_____
_____
_____
_____
_____
_____
_____
_____
_____
_____
_____
_____
_____

Appendix B
PERSONAL DEBT SCHEDULE

The Personal Debt Schedule is used to summarize all of your personal debt obligations and outlines every debt in detail with totals. It will help you see exactly what you have and will help you in managing your debt. Most importantly it can help you become debt free if it is used consistently in conjunction with your monthly budget. Complete the debt schedule separately in order to provide a clear and open financial view of each other's debt obligations. List all debt obligations and related information. Add and total the Monthly Payment, Current Balance and Value of Collateral columns. These totals will reflect your total outstanding debt obligations and the total monthly payments to all of your creditors. It also reflects the total value of the collateral associated with the outstanding debt obligations.

Creditor	Type	Rate	Mth Pymt	Term	Balance	Collateral Value
Total						

PERSONAL DEBT SCHEDULE NOTES

Appendix C

PERSONAL FINANCIAL STATEMENT (PFS) SHORT FORM

Complete the PFS separately to provide a clear and open financial picture of each other's assets, liabilities, and net worth. Fill in the amounts for each line item if applicable. Add and total the assets and liabilities. Net worth is calculated by subtracting total liabilities from total assets (Total Assets – Total Liabilities = Net Worth).

Assets	In even Dollars	Liabilities & Net Worth	In even Dollars
Cash on Hand in Banks		Bank Notes Payable	
Government Securities		Notes Payable (car loans)	
Accounts/Notes Receivables		Mortgage Payable (Personal Residence)	
Personal Residence		Life Insurance Loans	
Other Real Estate		Other Liabilities	
Cash Value Life Insurance			

Other Assets			
		TOTAL LIABILITIES	
		NET WORTH	
TOTAL ASSETS		**TOTAL LIABILITIES AND NET WORTH**	

PERSONAL FINANCIAL STATEMENT NOTES

Appendix D

CREDIT REPORTS

Obtaining your individual credit reports can be done by visiting www.annualcreditreport.com. This site allows consumers to obtain a free copy of each credit report once a year. This site was established by the three (3) main credit-reporting agencies: Equifax, Experian, and TransUnion, as required by federal law. Once on the website, simply follow the instructions. Be sure to pull all three reports because each report may not contain all the same credit information. Creditors do not have to report your credit information to all three credit bureau agencies. It is at the creditors' discretion as to which credit agency or agencies they subscribe in order report credit information of borrowers and credit applicants.

The credit rating agencies are listed below:

Equifax Credit: 800-685-1111 (www.equifax.com)

Experian: 888-397-3742 (www.experianplc.com)

TransUnion Corp: 800-916-8800 (www.transunion.com)

Once you and your partner have pulled all three reports, schedule a time to review and discuss them together. Check for accuracy and completeness. If there are errors, work together to clear them from your report(s).

CREDIT REPORT NOTES

www.ingramcontent.com/pod-product-compliance
Lightning Source LLC
Chambersburg PA
CBHW071129090426
42736CB00012B/2068